THE BIG IDEAS
OUR SILVER THREAD

By Dave Racer

Alethos Press LLC
St. Paul, MN

ALETHOS PRESS LLC
PO Box 600160
St. Paul, MN 55106

The Big Ideas: Our Silver Thread

ISBN 978-0-9777534-6-8

Printed in the U.S.A. by
Bethany Press International,
Bloomington, MN

http://www.alethospress.com
http://www.daveracer.com
        First Printing

Other Red, White and Blue Books

America's Creed
3 Fold Plan

TABLE OF CONTENTS

THE BIGGEST IDEA?

Is there God? Mankind has repeatedly asked and attempted to answer this question. America's Founding Fathers, however, expressed nearly universal acceptance of God as not only real, but active in the affairs of mankind.

Benjamin Franklin, considered a Deist, strongly defended the idea of God's reality, and more so, that God responds to the prayers of mankind.

Thomas Jefferson, another "Deist," in his 1805 Inaugural Address, specifically thanked God for His Providence, and asked all who listened to join with him in prayers for God's guidance.

The I AM. This is the Truth that underscores the Big Ideas.

THE NATION'S GUIDING PRINCIPLE

President John F. Kennedy, February 1961.

"This country was founded by men and women who were dedicated or came to be dedicated to two propositions: first, a strong religious conviction, and secondly a recognition that this conviction could flourish only under a system of freedom.

"I think it is appropriate that we pay tribute to this great constitutional principle which is enshrined in the First Amendment of the Constitution: the principle of religious independence, of religious liberty, of religious freedom. But I think it is also important that we pay tribute and acknowledge another great principle, and that is the principle of religious conviction. Religious freedom has no significance unless it is accompanied by conviction. And therefore the Puritans and the Pilgrims of my own section of New England, the Quakers of Pennsylvania, the Catholics of Maryland, the Presbyterians of North Carolina, the Methodists and the Baptists who came later, all shared these two great traditions which, like **silver threads**, have run through the warp and the woof of American history.

"No man who enters upon the office to which I have succeeded can fail to recognize how every president of the United States has placed special reliance upon his faith in God. Every president has taken comfort and courage when told…that the Lord "will be with thee. He will not fail thee nor forsake thee. Fear not—neither be thou dismayed." While they came from a wide variety of religious backgrounds and held a wide variety of religious beliefs, each of our presidents in his own way has placed a special trust in God. Those who were strongest intellectually were also strongest spiritually.

"…[L]et us go forth to lead this land that we love, joining in the prayer of General George Washington in 1783, 'that God would have you in His holy protection, that He would include the hearts of the citizens…to entertain a brotherly love and affection one for another…and finally that He would most graciously be pleased to dispose us all to do justice, to love mercy, and to demean ourselves with…the characteristics of the

Divine Author of our blessed religion, without an humble imitation of whose example we can never hope to be a happy nation.'

The guiding principle and prayer of this nation has been, is now, and shall ever be 'In God We Trust.'"

---

*...the Puritans and the Pilgrims of my own section of New England, the Quakers of Pennsylvania, the Catholics of Maryland, the Presbyterians of North Carolina, the Methodists and the Baptists who came later, all shared these two great traditions which, like **silver threads**, have run through the warp and the woof of American history.*

President John F. Kennedy

DEDICATION

Beginning in 1999, I enjoyed the challenge of teaching young people about the Big Ideas upon which our Founding Fathers built our nation. These future citizens were home-schooled by parents who were perplexed by the journey away from these ideas they had witnessed in our nation's government schools.

It is to my hundreds of students that I dedicate this book, hoping that the ideas represented herein will motivate them to fight to preserve and expand liberty.

WHAT'S THE BIG IDEA?

The founding fathers wrote in The Declaration of Independence about "self-evident truths." By this, they meant that observable, absolute truth does exist, and on these truths as foundation blocks, they could build both a philosophy for living and governing.

To discover truth, the founding fathers could have looked to human philosophers, as did the French revolutionaries. And indeed, they did consult contemporary and historical writers of their day, but not as primary sources. For primary sources, they looked to the Holy Bible.

Quite a long historical record exists to show how highly the founding fathers esteemed the Bible as primary truth, including the establishment of colleges and universities, state taxpayer support for churches and pastors, and federal government expense to print Bibles. (All of this occurred 150 years before the U.S. Supreme Court suddenly discovered that such government actions were "unconstitutional," even though it was the writers of the Constitution who committed those acts.) Innumerable references by America's founding fathers state clearly their belief that Christian faith is an essential element of freedom and foundational to self-governance.

There are many recorded references by our founding fathers to God and Jesus Christ, and the active role of the Divine in our governance. These references, however, are but a tiny representation of the predominance of Christianity in their day. There are far more references of this kind that rang from pre-revolutionary pulpits and fathers at family dinner tables during America's formative years. Though different denominations existed in the colonies, they all were united in their drive to live under the authority of God's law, and upon it, build man's law.

After the Bible, the founding fathers looked to Natural Law, Common Law, and written human works such as Magna Charta, Rutherford's Lex Rex, Locke's Two Treatises on Government, and Blackstone's Commentaries on the Laws of England.

NATURAL LAW CAME FIRST

Natural Law is God-breathed. It is the natural order of things, the knowledge of right and wrong and the aspects of human behavior informed by the "conscience." Paul wrote of it in Romans1 as that which is observed in nature, revelation of such to man making him aware of God. God created nature; God created Natural Law. He set the universe in motion, and it continues to operate by His laws – naturally.

One of those natural laws is that each facet of nature must be productive, or it dies.

God made man's mind. It is generally agreed among scholars that the mind has three facets: intellect, emotion and will. The intellect is that which is known; emotion, that which is felt; will, that which is done. These facets work in concert with each other. When they do not work together, that is, they work against each other, then the person becomes unstable.

Many scholars believe that the conscience is infallible; commending a person for doing right and condemning them for making wrong choices. Guidance of the conscience comes from the intellect, and God placed knowledge of His law in man; it is natural. If man violates this known revelation of God's law, the conscience condemns the man; and the will makes a choice. Man can choose to obey God's law or reject it.

Man's intellect is informed by exposure to knowledge, and to ideas – especially big ideas. As man accepts or rejects that knowledge, his conscience either commends or condemns him, but by a warped intellect – an intellect informed by erroneous knowledge – man can violate Natural Law, and fight against the conscience. But man can never escape his obligation to obey Natural Law, even when his intellect informs him otherwise. Run as far from it as he or she might, no one can escape the consequences of violations of Natural Law. That is why God provided His Son.

WRITTEN CODE

God gave His written code to Moses. Condensed into 10 commandments, these provided the outline for a sustainable and predictable system of law.

Those commandments dealt with two aspects of human life: man's relationship with the Creator and man's relationship with man. Our "religion" is encapsulated in the first four command-

ments and our civil and criminal laws – the government – in the remaining six commandments.

In terms of human governance, God separated religion from State control when He set aside the tribe of Levi to serve as priests to Jacob's family. When those who were not Levites attempted to cross the line and perform priestly responsibilities, God judged them – even killed them. It cost Saul his kingship. But God subjected all of the tribes of Jacob to His precepts, in the establishment of civil law and criminal law, and observance of faith's requirements. God gave His Law as a way of life for His people, and to follow His Law would result in peace and prosperity; to ignore or fail to follow it would result in destruction and death (see Deut. 28).

Since the ill-advised Everson v. USA (1947) Supreme Court decision, a body of law has developed that tries to enforce the "separation of church and state." Those who believe that this is a foundational government principle could seize on the Ten Commandments to prove their point. They could further point to the separation between the Levites and the other 12 tribes, just as described above. They may suggest God saw the logic in separating these two factions. They would be right, in the context of ancient Jewish society.

America, however, is not patterned on the ancient Jewish rule of law nor its governments. Rather, it is a Republic built primarily on Protestant Christian principles, reason and Common Law. The greatest difference between the ancient Jew and modern American is that we do not have judges appointed by God nor kings that He anointed. We elect our leaders – we are the kings in America. So no one can point to the dichotomy between commands I-IV, and V-X, and the division in Jewish law to justify separation of church and state.

Common Law embodies the practice of civil and criminal law that grew during more than a millennia as England continued to build its own nationhood. Common Law precedents preceded Magna Charta and the idea that government could only be established by consent of the governed.

Records of English Kings as early as the Fifth Century showed a consistent reliance on the Roman Catholic Church to define portions of Common Law as they pertained to the moral actions of English citizens, and to assist in adjudication of claims between citizens. In that way, Catholic teachings as they touched civil and criminal law, became incorporated into Common Law. For centuries, Common Law, the Bible, Magna Charta and the laws of various Kings (themselves subject to Holy Writ) served as the basis of English law.

The founding fathers adopted Common Law (except those portions that dealt with the English monarchy). They also studied and relied upon the work of lawyers such as Sir Edmund Coke and William Blackstone, men who distinguished themselves in the practice, development and codification of Common Law. Blackstone, whose commentaries became the primary source of America's earliest legal systems, studied Coke. Coke served as the chief prosecutor in the King's court during the early 1600s.

All of this is to say that America's legal and governing foundations are big ideas, self-evident truths; ideas both profound and simple, and as such, immensely powerful. America's founding fathers built our legal and governing systems upon a strong foundation. Modern American courts have incredibly declared, by implication, that the founding fathers were wrong and in fact, so misguided so that they violated their own Constitution. The Supreme Court began stepping away from original intent almost from the beginning, but it took 150 years for it to first assault America's Christian foundation, and slowly pull out its cornerstone, leaving us now with a legal system based only on the whim and fancy of a ruling elite, the oligarchy called the United States Supreme Court.

ALEXIS DE TOCQUEVILLE

 "The Americans combine the notions [Big Ideas] of Christianity and of liberty so intimately in their minds, that it is impossible to make them conceive of one without the other."

From his book, *Religion and Democracy*, 1835.

SOME OF THOSE BIG IDEAS

The founding fathers were able to balance the idealism found in striving toward big ideas at the same time as coping with real world problems – they were realists. The 10 Commandments clearly enough stated, "Thou shalt not kill," a self-evident truth. The founding fathers knew better than to govern themselves in the simple hope that every person would obey that commandment; they created criminal laws to punish murderers. Laws, they saw, bound the spirit of man in such a way that allowed mankind to live in peace. Yet the practical failings of humans never kept the founding fathers from faith in big ideas. Rather than treating them as elusive, they saw how ideas and actions were interwoven in a tapestry of peace and prosperity.

Man is, by nature, a spiritual creation; That is a big idea. God breathed His spirit into man at creation. If man will not believe in the true God, he will invent one – idols, earth, the environment, politics.

Procreation is a big idea. When God ordered the universe, He instructed Adam and Eve to bear children and fill the earth. Not to do so would have resulted in the death of the human race. The same is true of all types of life; if it doesn't reproduce, it dies. Violation of any aspect of God's law re-

sults in judgment, but none more severe than to fail to procreate. Any official government policy that opposes this big idea stands to put at jeopardy the survival of not only the government, but of the species. Governments must promote the procreation of human life and protect against those forces that threaten it.

The nuclear family is a big idea. "Family First" would have been a perfect campaign motto for a congressional candidate in 1787. Everyone would have known what it meant, and it would remain so until the late 1960s. God said children were to honor their parents, and if they did, He promised them a long life. The first and most important unit of government is the family. Though the Declaration makes no mention of family being an unalienable right (one suspects that in 1776 no

one would have been foolish enough to challenge such a notion) it does identify life, liberty and the pursuit of happiness as primary. Human life springs from the union of a man and woman; liberty and self-restraint are learned at home; virtue and self-reliance come from strong families. Governments must protect the institution of the family.

The ultimate value of human life is a big idea. God said we should not murder, and to prove His own love for us, He allowed His own Son, though completely innocent, to be murdered in place of us. The founding fathers wrote of human life as being inalienable, something over which no man has authority, save when a person waives that right by murdering others. Sometimes, protecting life means sacrificing some lives, a fact very well known to those who have fought in America's wars. Law and American justice must protect human life against all those who threaten it.

Sexual purity and faithfulness to one's spouse – and family – are big ideas. God said we are not to commit adultery, and as such, requires fidelity and sexual purity among humans. Laws that punish sexual deviance and protect purity help preserve the order and security of society. Sexual license may be private in terms of an intimate act, but it is not private by nature. Immoral private sexual acts – adultery, fornication, sodomy – have negative societal impact, whether in terms of family breakdown, out of wedlock pregnancy, communicable disease or negative affects on the spirit of a community. Ultimately, sexual license contributes to societal breakdown and death. Most Americans agree that governments do not belong in the privacy of the bedroom with adults. Yet, governments have a vital interest in promoting and protecting moral purity.

The right to own and use property is a big idea. God said we are not to steal another's property. The founding fathers, as expressed by John Locke, and later, in the US Constitution, saw property as an inalienable right. As such, governments were to respect and protect private property.

**Volunteers Welcome
Check in at Office**

This included real estate and buildings, but also, that which could be earned by the sweat of one's brow: salaries, wages, investments and the like. A primary responsibility of government is to enforce contracts, and protect the rights of people to gain, hold, own, sell and profit by property.

Telling the truth is a big idea. God said we are not to lie. Lying breaks down the security of a family, community, state and nation. We must be able to rely on each other telling the truth in order to conduct our daily affairs. But telling the truth also assumes that truth exists and can be known; truth cannot be relative or situational. Truth must be truth (and that is a huge idea). Governments must protect truth-tellers and punish liars.

Right motivations toward owning and using things and holding close certain relationships is a big idea. Paul told the Corinthian Christians to be "cheerful givers." He described a society where wealthier members needed to give to help less wealthy members, in fact, reminding them that some day, the poorer ones might return

13

the favor. Such an attitude stands in stark contrast with being a greedy or covetous person. God says we are not to covet; we are not to take or be envious of what is rightfully someone else's. Covetousness is rooted in self-centeredness and leads to the disregard of God's law. A nation filled with covetous people would be a dangerous place to live. A government that moves from protecting private property to transferring private property from one class of people to another would be a government based on power and greed, not based on law. Governments must guard against policies that encourage and act on covetous behavior and worse yet, discourage charity.

Separation of the Earth from the Waters.

"Then God said, "Let there be a firmament in the midst of the waters..." Gen. 1:6a

AS IT WAS IN
THE BEGINNING

At America's beginning, the founding fathers built their new government on the big ideas of worship of God, prohibiting the government from regulating religious faith, and establishing a constitution based on the moral teachings of the 10 Commandments and Common Law. Common Law found its roots in the various writings of the apostles, the gospels, Old Testament writings and the traditions of the Christian leaders of its earliest days.

When the Northwest Ordinance stated, "religion, morality and knowledge" were requirements for mankind's happiness, they pointed to the big ideas found in the Holy Scriptures.

When President George Washington spoke to the Delaware Indian Chiefs on May 12, 1779, he said, "What students would learn in American schools above all is the religion of Jesus Christ." President Washington said elsewhere, "It is impossible to rightly govern the world without God and the Bible."

15

God's Word remains static, stable, predictable, unchangeable. Man's law, by contrast, historically reacts to the whim of powerful rulers, and so it was until man's law, as expressed in the U.S. Constitution, reflected God's Law. Man's law was arbitrary and brutal until tamed by God's Law and codified into our written Constitution. To see today's Constitution as somehow based on Reason, or the Enlightenment, majority rule, science, or human philosophy, is to have removed America from her foundation.

All forms of government are wholly dependent on the foundation on which they stand. It is not that we cannot have government based on Science, or Reason, or Sustainable Development, or Animal Rights, or any other big ideas. It is that such governments so construed will not be republics that maximize human liberty and protect human life. They may more likely be powerful centralized governments dependent solely on the whim of ruling elitists.

Dr. David Noebel writes in *Understanding the Times* about big ideas that stand in conflict. He writes about a "Christian Worldview" as opposed to a "Humanist Worldview," or "Marxism-Leninism" or "New Age" philosophies. It is possible to summarize this conflict simply: God or no God. Either Genesis 1:1 is right – "In the beginning, God created…" – or it is wrong. If it is wrong, and the truth is that "In the beginning, gas created…," then the form of government seen at America's beginning will no longer work (in fact, it would have to be argued that it never did work).

If the big idea that dominates American government is "no God," then by necessity, individual liberty and choice must be limited by a powerful government. Big government becomes a friend, while personal choice is sacrificed for the good of the whole. The big ideas foundational to our traditional form of government must change. Our new big ideas would include:

• A family can be any organizational form where people live together for any reason.

• The government is also the parent.

• We have choice to kill our innocent unborn children, but must stop executing murderers – and by all means, we must extend grace to terrorists.

The Prayer at Valley Forge painted by Henry Brueckner, engraved by John C. McRae. George Washington is shown praying under trees with his military camp in the background.

17

• Sexual preferences must be tolerated, promoted and accepted. All genders must be sexually liberated (we must understand that there are at least 64 genders and accept them all).

• Individual use of property must be ordered by the needs of the community, and growth must be sustainable.

• All persons should expect to live in a state of equality of things; no person should ever go hungry or be allowed to over-indulge.

• All children can learn everything. No child should be left behind. Equal outcomes for everyone.

• Government should establish an accepted level of prosperity for all, and redistribute assets as needed to maintain a proper balance.

• Humans are created by their environment and subject to it, and therefore, manipulation of the environment is the chief role of government.

A government built on these liberal principles cannot continue to claim to be one that promotes individual freedom. Rather, freedom that presumes these principles to be true deems that all individual decisions will have to be by a central government. It is inevitable.

LIBERALS & CONSERVATIVES

The big ideas expressed by those who care about political and governmental issues ultimately draw the line between modern day liberal and conservative thought. Dictionary definitions of these terms are no longer useful.

LIBERALS

One group of political thinkers – liberals – sees all truth as relative. The liberal's big idea is that big ideas are always evolving, and so is truth. Science and reason must always trump religious faith since nothing can be "known" by faith. Since scientists and philosophers are constantly discovering new truths and ideas, every rule and law must be evolving. Since everything evolves, everything is at the mercy of environmental factors.

By environmental factors, liberals mean two things. They mean those actions and attitudes that impinge on a person, forcing them into a set

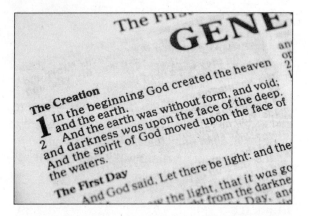

The two primary competing ideologies in the United States are driven by their view of Creation. If God created man and breathed the Spirit of Life into him; if God plays an active role in the life of man; then man is inner-directed.

If evolution created man, then man has no rational inner-drive by which to guide himself, since he is the sum total and victim of his environment.

How one views God and His role in creation, and in sustaining life, makes all the difference in how a person views the factors that energize man.

of actions and reactions. Or they mean the physical environment, that is, Gaia – the earth mother.

Liberals see individuals as at the mercy of the actions and attitudes of others. Most often, others' actions and attitudes work to the detriment of certain protected classes of people – the victim classes. Victims include children, sick, elderly and any minority group not identified as Christian. Liberals, in fact, see Christians as an environmental element that works against the rest of the people, and all the more, if they are Caucasian Christians.

Liberals also see the natural environment as a big idea; so big, in fact, that human society must be organized to maximize the peace and protection of the environment. Liberals see humans as Evil Ones who attack, denigrate and destroy Earth.

Since humans are creations of their environment (and the chief antagonist of Gaia), then it is the object of government to manipulate,

21

create and protect the environment in such a manner as to best suit the needs of human victim groups; all the time making sure the water, air and dirt are kept clean (although Gaia comes first).

Liberal politicians, then, are the big idea people who are in charge of manipulating the environment for the common good.

Liberals see people as thermometers, who reflect the impact of factors over which they have no control. The people need liberal politicians to make life bearable.

Incredibly, liberals see it as wrong that government should impose on people absolute law based on a system of foundational beliefs, yet at the same time, see the need for a strong central government in order to protect the people as a whole.

Liberals say they oppose a rigid moral code; they accuse conservatives of "imposing their morals on others." Teaching children how to put a condom on a banana, however, they see as a positive manipulation of the environmental factors that otherwise will drive teenagers to have premarital sex; maybe even with members of their own gender. Liberals do not see that they impose morals on anyone; what they endorse is for everyone's good.

Liberals are quick to defend freedom of the press, but believe religion must be erased from the public debate. Author Ann Coulter wrote, "Liberals hate religion because politics is a religious substitute for liberals and they can't stand the competition." In truth, liberals are dogmatic and rigid while imposing their own morality – which conservatives label "immorality" – on others.

CONSERVATIVES

The modern conservative sees that absolute truth exists and can be counted on as guidance for life's decisions. Even secular conservatives hold to certain basic principles as facts, whereas religious conservatives look to the Bible and religious instruction to find the big ideas upon which they base their lives.

Conservatives see that they are mostly in control of their own lives. They can choose to do good or evil, work or not work, obey the law or break it. They are free to accept God on His terms, try to set their own terms, or reject Him altogether.

Likewise, conservatives recognize the effect of environmental factors on their own lives. As such, they can choose to change those factors,

accept them, or move on to a different environ-
ment.

Conservatives use external factors (actions
and attitudes of others) as a springboard to their
own success. When they and countless others like
them are successful, everyone benefits. Best of all,
this is done efficiently, without government inter-
ference and cost.

Conservatives see the natural environment
as a great laboratory for ideas, recreation, human
enjoyment and use. They are unlikely purposely
to poison their own wells, or their neighbors'.
They are stewards of the environment, not its vic-
tims.

Conservatives resent when the government
tries to be their nanny or conscience. They need
neither, since they are, in a human sense, self-suf-

ficient. And Christian conservatives know they will ultimately answer to God and so, are fully reliant on Him for His gracious daily gift of life and sustenance. They look to family, friends and church for support, but only when they want it; not when someone else says it is good for them (as others define "good").

Conservatives see the object of government is to protect their right to become what they want to be. Generally, conservatives see government as a necessary organization for certain aspects of life – transportation, military defense, protecting and enforcing contracts, etc.

Conservatives disdain the idea of the government redistributing private property for some greater good that others have defined. They feel perfectly competent to find needs and meet them on their own, without the government taking their hard-earned money. They practice charity when they are lead to do so, not because the Department of Human Services demands it of them.

Conservatives are like thermostats. When the environment gets un-comfortable, they work to change the setting, either cooling it down or warming it up. They see themselves as in control of their destiny; though religious conservatives ac-

25

knowledge God as the ultimate Sovereign to Whom they answer for each decision.

Religious conservatives do not live as libertarians. Libertarians see themselves as entrusted with their own liberty. Rather, religious conservatives live as trustees of the liberty bestowed on them by God; with a charge from Him to live in accordance with His Big Ideas (see above). Central government has purpose because God so defined it, and it has limits for the same reason.

Conservatives do not attempt to force their morals on anyone. Rather, they prefer to live by the moral standards God established. In reality, man will live by either God's moral standards or man's; either way, someone's morals will be imposed.

CAVEAT

The terms liberal and conservative really do not well define any dominant political camp. People are naturally a mixture of thoughts, ideas and persuasions. They may be overly pious as it concerns family and gender relations – even ultra conservative – while placing trust in centralized government to provide economic security – ultra liberal.

The pro-life union worker may be conservative about protecting the lives of unborn children, but still demand that government reign in corporations and insure lucrative pensions. The pro-family conservative middle manager may resent homosexuals trying to gain status as "normal," but expect that government will provide Social Security and Medicare until their dying day. The pro-decency conservative homemaker may protest the filth that spews from daily TV shows, but demand more government spending on public education.

It seems that many modernists, whether conservative or liberal, or in combination as most of us are, have lost sight of the big ideas that formed America's foundations. Therefore, it is common for many well-meaning people of faith to follow as if blind, even embracing the big ideas of those forces that steal their freedoms and run their lives in contradiction to their own perceived beliefs and desires. They support those liberal politicians who, at their root, never trust people of faith and, by their actions, enforce a form of law repugnant to Christians.

CORPORATE VS. INDIVIDUAL APPLICATIONS

America's founding fathers fought against government tyranny of the spirit. James Madison and Thomas Jefferson opposed the collection of taxes to pay for churches and preachers not because they were against belief in Christ; they opposed government forcing a preferred form of faith on citizens. Each citizen, they saw, needed to choose for himself which form of faith to follow. This would best be accomplished, they believed, if federal and state governments did not choose an official religion. Yet, at no time did they suggest that government had no interest in promoting religious faith – quite the contrary.

The founding fathers saw corporate religious faith, especially the Christian faith, as a requirement for maintenance of freedom. That fact made it possible for them to refer to self-evident truths, which were accepted by faith even if observable in nature.

The truth is that no society can, over the long run, successfully force a set of beliefs onto all of its citizens, but it can highly affect what they believe. Even if those truths are Biblically based, governments cannot force people to believe them, but governments can go a long way in negatively affecting religious belief, and to do so requires replacing the idea of self-evident truths with relativism, hedonism and humanism.

If schools that are paid for by the government ("public" schools) choose for curriculum certain ideas as seen through a humanist worldview, then the students they produce will see big ideas as relativistic. Big ideas are what each person defines, but the idea definers will be those who see mankind as god, and see God as irrelevant. In such a society, there can be no room for foundational truth, beyond the belief that all truth is evolutional.

SHARED COMMON BELIEFS A PREREQUISITE

To continue to operate, governments must rely on certain shared beliefs. If those beliefs are informed by Natural Law, Common Law, Mosaic Law, Declarationism, and original intent of the Constitution, there will be maximum freedom. If governing beliefs are informed only by science and reason that is not informed by faith, freedom will eventually give way to rule by might.

A nation consists of millions of citizens, each making

"The secret of my success? It is simple. It is found in the Bible. 'In all thy ways acknowledge Him and He shall direct thy paths."
George Washington Carver

"Religion ... is the opium of the people." **Karl Marx** wrote in *A Contribution to the Critique of Hegel's Philosophy of Right*

decisions informed by something. It remains the responsibility of those of us who trust in the big ideas – self-evident truths – embraced by the founding fathers, to compete in the marketplace of ideas. We have that right; we have that responsibility. We must inform those within our circle of influence about self-evident truths, the big ideas created by God. That is the way we will preserve and protect our freedoms.

In 2 Timothy 2:2, Paul writes about how believers were to spread the Gospel. He said that faithful men (humans) were to teach other faithful humans. One tells another who tells another. We who believe in the Creator God must use this same formula to contest for big ideas and pass along truth. To do so will change society.

BIG IDEAS MATTER IN BIG WAYS

Time will reveal who wins the battle of big ideas here on earth.

Biblical Christians (those who have actually read and studied the Bible) know that in time, God's victory will be evident to everyone; in fact, He has always been winning. At the end, though, God will bring with Him all who have understood the biggest idea of all; that God is love, God sent His son to redeem fallen man, and in so doing, gave man all the big ideas he needs to live what Christ called the "abundant life."

While we live here on this earth, especially in the United States, it is not so clear which big ideas will win. Apathy and Ignorance, those dreadful twin human characteristics, infect both liberals and conservatives. In some ways, though, conservatives are more prone to dropping out of the big idea debate. They would rather be left alone. Without Christian conservative salt and light, the big ideas of darkness will ultimately and naturally evolve into a government system run by might, not by right.

When right can no longer be defined as God's big ideas, but rather, as the ideas evolving out of man's reason and study, then human rights will naturally give way to a set of government-imposed rights. Such can only be the case because there will be no consensus of rights by the people. If rights are arbitrary, then so too is government, and only an ever stronger hand is able to rule the people.

Each generation must rediscover and redefine its foundational big ideas. It remains unknown which ideas today's generation will look to as foundational, but it is crucial to ask and instruct them.

We the people established the Constitution in part to pass along the blessings of liberty to our posterity. That means our progeny must know, understand and incorporate into their own belief systems the big ideas that matter for eternity. The alternative is to sell out their future for rule by the strongest humans, rather than by God's meek champions.

> "So great is my veneration for the Bible, that the earlier my children begin to read it the more confident will be my hopes that they will prove useful citizens to their country and respectable members of society."

President John Quincy Adams

Dr. Benjamin Rush
Signer of the Declaration of Independence in a
letter to Thomas Jefferson

I have always considered Christian-
ity as the strong ground of republi-
canism. The spirit is opposed, not
only to the splendor, but even to the
very forms of monarchy, and many of
its precepts have for their objects re-
publican liberty and equality as well
as simplicity, integrity, and economy
in government. It is only necessary
for republicanism to ally itself to the
Christian religion to overturn all the
corrupted political and religious in-
stitutions in the world.

ABOUT THE AUTHOR

Dave Racer, MLitt

Dave is an author, speaker, and publisher. He is the CEO of Alethos Press LLC, the founding President of The Declaration Project, and former President and Chairman of the Constitutional Educational Foundation.

Dave hosted a Twin Cities-based radio talk show (*The Dave Racer Show*) for more than six years, and is a frequent guest on talk and news shows. During the 1980s, he published a monthly newspaper, *Dave Racer's Minnesota Report*, and served as Executive Director of Minnesota Proposition 180.

Dave has been a four-time endorsed candidate for the Minnesota State Legislature, and served as campaign manager for the Menning for Governor Committee (1985-1986). In 1995-1998,

Dave served as the National Campaign Manager for Alan Keyes for President.

Since 1999, Dave has taught high school aged home school students about American government and politics.

Since 2005, Dave has focused on health care system reform, and is a national speaker and writer on the topic. Besides his books about health reform, Dave has authored numerous articles and papers.

In 2009, Oxford Graduate School awarded Dave the Master of Letters Degree. He wrote his thesis on comprehensive reform of the United States' health care system.

Dave and his wife Rosanne, married in 1967, have five adult children, and live in the Twin Cities. At this writing, they have three grandchildren.

For more information, see:

http://www.daveracer.com

Write to Dave Racer

Alethos Press LLC
PO Box 600160
St Paul, MN 55106

TO ORDER MORE OF THESE BOOKS OR OTHER RED, WHITE & BLUE BOOKS

Go to: http://www.alethospress.com

Or contact

Alethos Press LLC
PO Box 600160
St Paul, MN 55106

651.340.1911